P·I·C·T·U·R·E·P·E·D·I·A

NOTE TO PARENTS

This book is part of PICTUREPEDIA, a completely
new kind of information series for children.
Its unique combination of pictures and words
encourages children to use their eyes to discover and
explore the world, while introducing them to a wealth
of basic knowledge. Clear, straightforward text
explains each picture thoroughly and provides
additional information about the topic.

'Looking it up' becomes an easy task with
PICTUREPEDIA, an ideal first reference for all types of
schoolwork. Because PICTUREPEDIA is also entertaining,
children will enjoy reading its words and looking
at its pictures over and over again. You can encourage and
stimulate further inquiry by helping your child
pose simple questions for the whole family to
'look up' and answer together.

INSECTS AND SPIDERS

DK

A DORLING KINDERSLEY BOOK
Conceived, edited and designed by DK Direct Limited

Consultant Paul Hillyard

Project Editor Rosemary McCormick
Art Editor Richard Clemson
Designer Marianne Markham

Series Editor Sarah Phillips
Series Art Editor Paul Wilkinson

Picture Researcher Lorna Ainger

Production Manager Ian Paton
Production Assistant Harriet Maxwell

Editorial Director Jonathan Reed
Design Director Ed Day

First published in Great Britain in 1993
by Dorling Kindersley Limited
9 Henrietta Street
London WC2E 8PS

A CIP catalogue record for this
book is available from the British Library.

ISBN 0-7513-5087-7

Reproduced by Colourscan, Singapore
Printed and bound in Italy by Graphicom

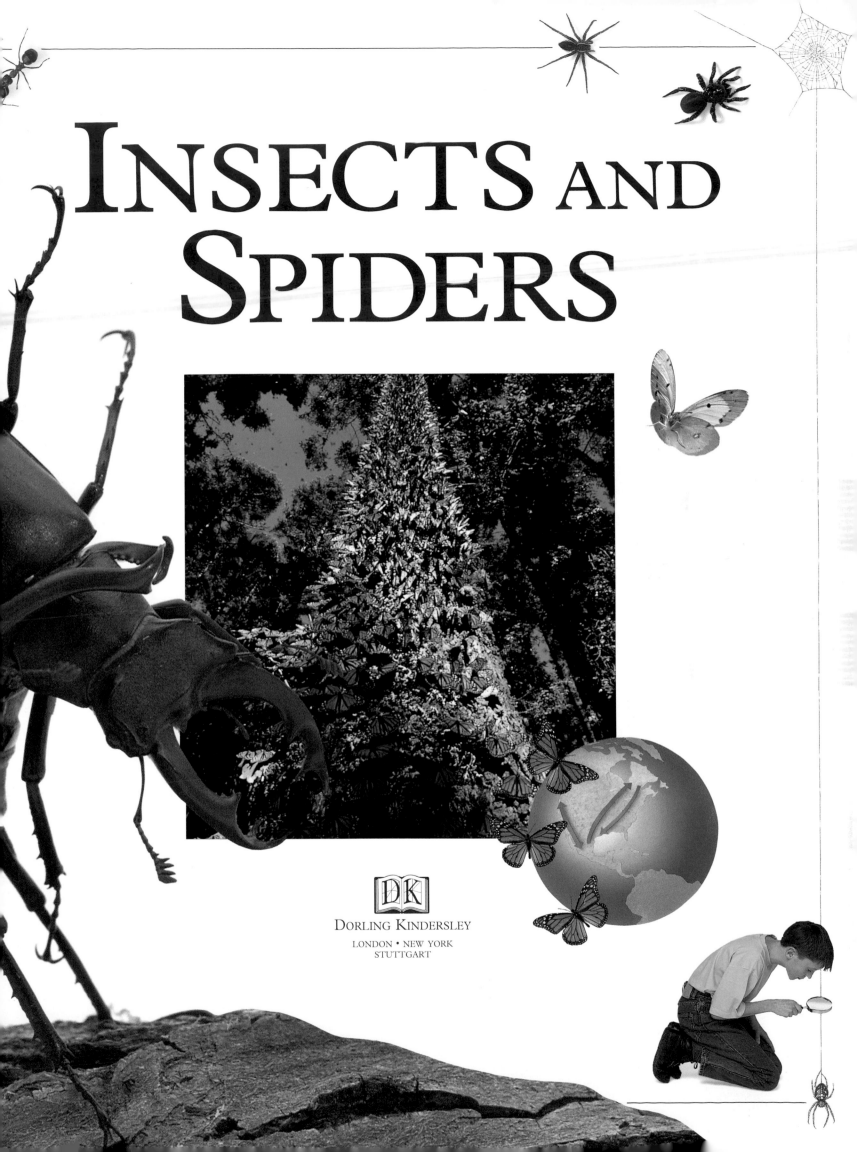

INSECTS AND SPIDERS

DK

DORLING KINDERSLEY

LONDON • NEW YORK
STUTTGART

CONTENTS

WHAT IS AN INSECT?

Head

Thorax

Abdomen

Scientists think that there are more than a million known types of insect in the world and that there are many more waiting to be discovered. Most insects are rarely seen. They live hidden away from view, creeping through undergrowth, building homes in gardens and forests. But some, occasionally, come to live in our homes.

Insect Features
Not all creepy crawlies are insects. Insects are identified partly by the way their body is divided into three parts – a head, thorax and abdomen.

All insects have simple eyes which are sensitive to light.

True Bugs
Even though we sometimes call insects bugs, many of them are not. But there are creatures that are true bugs. Bugs can be identified by their mouthparts which are formed into moveable beaks used to pierce and suck food. Bugs' forewings are always hard at the base and soft at the tip.

Adult insects use their antennae for feeling and 'smelling'.

This insect also has two large compound eyes. Insects with compound eyes can see images and spot even the smallest movement.

Eat Up
Insect mouthparts are specially designed according to their diet.

Beetles bite and chew their food. They also have jaws to grasp prey.

Flies spit on their food to dissolve it. Then they suck it up.

Butterflies have a proboscis which is used to suck up nectar.

Mosquitoes pierce skin and suck blood.

Honeybees eat with a wide-tipped proboscis called a 'honey spoon'.

Staying Power

There were insects on Earth long before the dinosaurs arrived. The first insects came from the steamy swamps of long ago. Some were man-sized monsters, but over the ages they have become smaller and smaller.

350–280 million years ago

280–65 million years ago

65 million years ago to present day

Ordering Insects

Scientists have divided insects up into large groups, or orders. Similar-looking insects are in the same order.

Butterfly

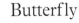

Beetle

This is a jewelled frog beetle, which lives in the tropical rainforest.

Most adult insects have wings.

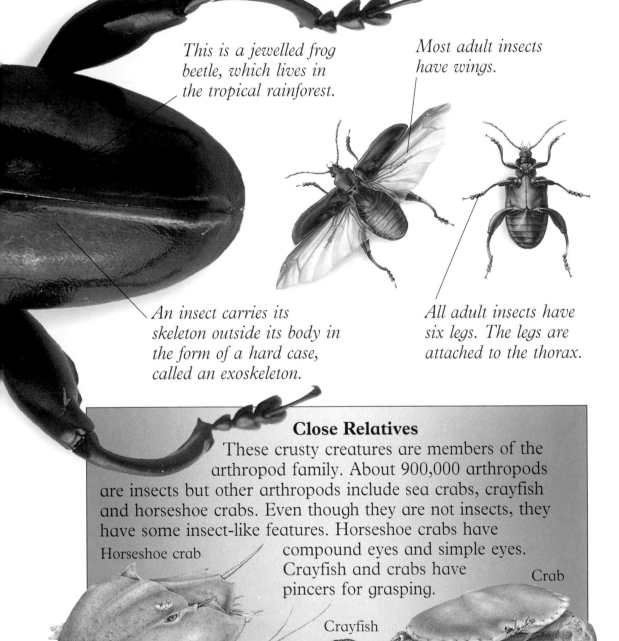

An insect carries its skeleton outside its body in the form of a hard case, called an exoskeleton.

All adult insects have six legs. The legs are attached to the thorax.

Dragonfly

Wasp

Close Relatives

These crusty creatures are members of the arthropod family. About 900,000 arthropods are insects but other arthropods include sea crabs, crayfish and horseshoe crabs. Even though they are not insects, they have some insect-like features. Horseshoe crabs have compound eyes and simple eyes. Crayfish and crabs have pincers for grasping.

Horseshoe crab

Crab

Crayfish

Grasshopper

FLIES

You have probably seen a house fly zooming around your kitchen. Most people think of flies as pests – annoying little creatures that buzz around us, bite us, walk on our food and spread disease. But in other ways, flies are a necessary and useful part of our world. They help to pollinate plants and are eaten by a variety of other animals.

A hoverfly taking off

Sensitive Flies
Flies have surprisingly strong senses. This means they have very good eyesight, and a keen sense of taste and smell.

Flies have two large compound eyes which see colours and shapes.

Many flies, like the house fly, have small antennae.

When the fly finds liquid food, it simply sucks it up. If it finds solid food, the fly first dissolves it with special juices.

Nice to See You!
Our eyes have just one rounded lens. A house fly has thousands of six-sided lenses and each lens sees a part, or piece, of a bigger picture. When a house fly looks at you, it sees you as different pieces.

At the end of a fly's mouth are two pads that look like lips.

When landing, a fly will put its front legs up over its head.

Then it grabs hold of the surface and flips its body upside down.

Special Feet
Flies can walk on the ceiling because they have two sharp claws on each foot. These are used to grip hold of the surface. They also have cup-shaped suction pads which stick to smooth surfaces.

True flies don't have back wings. Instead they have little bumps which look like drumsticks. These are called halteres. They help the fly to balance as it flies.

A house fly makes a buzzing sound. The buzz is caused by the fly's wings beating amazingly fast – about 200 times per second!

Flies have hairy, jointed legs. The hairs sense movement and this helps the fly stay out of danger.

Claws

Suction pads

Flittering Flies

South American mydas fly

Robber fly

Hover fly

Stalk-eyed fly

Horse fly

Crane fly

There are about 10,000 known types of crane fly in the world. In England, they are sometimes called daddy-longlegs.

BEETLES

There are more species of beetle in the world than any other kind of animal. It is thought there are at least 300,000. Most are plant-eaters but some battling beetles attack and eat other insects and are quite ferocious. Beetles can be pests because they eat valuable crops. But mostly they are helpful to us because they eat dead plants and animals and return them to the earth as important nutrients.

Ready for Battle
A beetle's hard outer casing acts like a protective armour.

Forewing

Take That!
These fighting beetles are stag beetles. They get their name because male stag beetles have large 'horns'. These are really large jaws that are used for fighting like the antlers of a real stag. Males fight to defend their territory.

The tough, black wing-case protects the delicate hind wings.

Hind wing

The beetle's claws help it to grip.

Special Friend
Ladybirds are beetles too. Not all beetles can fly but ladybirds can. They use their hind wings to fly.

Little and Large
The smallest known insect in the world is the feather-winged beetle. It is so small it can sit on a pinhead. The Hercules beetle is thought to be the longest beetle in the world. It can grow up to 17 centimetres long!

Valiant Beetles

Rove beetle

Tortoise beetle

Giraffe beetle

If it's attacked, it fires off a mixture of burning chemicals.

Bombardier beetle

Fighting males lift each other off the ground. They do this by grasping their opponent around the middle.

Night Lights
Fireflies are not really flies, they are beetles. At night, the females put on a light show as they flash their tails to attract a mate. They are able to do this because they have a special chemical in their body.

Hard, antler-like jaws.

Beetles have palps to help them sense food.

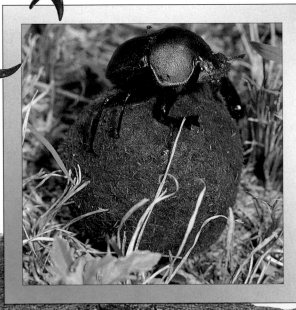

Beetle storing dung

Roll Over
Dung beetles go to a lot of trouble to find a safe and nutritious home for their young. They collect animal dung and roll it into large balls. They roll the dung balls all the way to their underground homes. There they lay their eggs in the dung. When the beetle larvae hatch they discover a tasty meal in front of them!

CATERPILLARS

Caterpillars are like tiny eating machines. They spend most of their time chomping on leaves. Caterpillars are actually the young of butterflies and moths. They hatch from the eggs the adult female has laid on plants. With constant eating they get bigger and bigger, until they are ready to change into butterflies and moths.

A New Skin
Caterpillar skin cannot stretch. So as it gets larger, the caterpillar breaks out of its skin. Underneath is a new, larger skin which will last until the caterpillar needs to moult again.

Caterpillars produce silk from special glands and force it out through a spinneret under the head.

The front three pairs of legs are called thoracic legs, and are used for walking and clasping.

Caterpillars have twelve tiny simple eyes, called ocelli, on their head.

Hatching Out
The butterfly's eggs are laid on the underside of a leaf.

The egg gets darker as the caterpillar prepares to hatch.

The caterpillar bites its way out and then pulls itself free of the eggshell.

The caterpillar's head is armed with a pair of stout jaws called mandibles.

Caterpillars test food and guide it to their mouth with mouthparts called maxillary palps.

The body is divided into 13 segments.

The first meal is the eggshell, which is full of good food.

onderful Caterpillars

aterpillars can be hairy, spiny d have unusual shapes.

Tiger moth caterpillar

bbage white caterpillar

Emperor moth caterpillar

Puss moth caterpillar

Like most insects, aterpillars breathe hrough openings alled spiracles.

The five pairs of stumpy, sucker-like legs are called prolegs. The caterpillar uses them for clinging onto plant stalks.

Silkworms

Silk is produced by most moth caterpillars. But the finest silk is produced by the large white moth caterpillar, often known as a silkworm. After the caterpillars have spun themselves into a silken cocoon, they are put into boiling water. The silk is removed and spun into threads to create material for clothes.

Masters of Disguise

To avoid being eaten, some caterpillars have developed crafty disguises. The hawk-moth caterpillar looks like a deadly snake, the lobster moth looks like a raised lobster's claw and the common sailer looks like a shrivelled leaf.

Hawk-moth

Lobster moth

Common sailer

Excuse Me, I'm Changing

To become adult moths, most moth caterpillars spin themselves a cocoon using silk, which comes out of the spinneret. Inside, they undergo astonishing physical changes.

13

BUTTERFLIES

Butterflies are perhaps the most beautiful of all insects. It is amazing to think that a fat, leaf-eating caterpillar can become a brightly coloured, fluttering creature of the air. The change happens in the butterfly chrysalis. The caterpillar's body is broken down and completely changed. After about four weeks, a fully formed butterfly emerges.

Time to Wake Up
The butterfly comes out of the chrysalis in three stages. During this time it is very open to attack by hungry birds or spiders.

1. No longer a caterpillar, a beautiful butterfly comes out of the chrysalis with its wings crumpled up.

Monarchs on the Move
Most butterflies are born, live and die in one place. But when winter comes to the eastern and western coasts of North America, thousands of red monarchs fly south to the warmth of California and Mexico. When warm weather returns to their first home, they fly north again.

ppy Landings

clouded yellow butterfly comes
to land on a thistle. Butterfly
ght is more controlled than it
ks. The insect is able to
ange course instantly and
ke sudden landings.

*Butterflies feed through a tube
called a proboscis. This is
coiled up when not in use.*

*Butterflies
have clubbed
antennae.*

In the Background

Butterflies make a tasty meal for birds.
But if they are able to blend in with
their background, they may avoid
being eaten. The open wings of the
Indian leaf butterfly
have a striking orange
patterning. But when
its wings are closed,
the butterfly looks
exactly like an old,
dry leaf.

Wings open

*Wings closed,
resting on leaf*

Brilliant Butterflies

*2. The butterfly must stay
still for some hours, as blood
is pumped into the wing veins
to stretch the wings. Later it
holds its wings apart to
let them harden.*

*3. When its wings have
hardened, the butterfly
is ready to fly off to find
its first meal of nectar.*

Male bird-wing butterfly

Glass swallowtail butterfly

88 butterfly

Scaly Wings

The wings of both butterflies
and moths are made up of
tiny scales, which overlap like
the tiles on a roof. Bright
colours can either be used to
attract a mate, or to warn
predators that the butterfly,
or moth, is not good to eat.

Cramer's blue morpho butterfly

MOTHS

Most moths are night-fliers and their strong sense of smell and hearing make them well suited to a night-time existence. They can easily find their way through darkness and although attracted to light, they are dazed by it. Moths rest by day, and many are coloured to look like tree bark or leaves so that they cannot be spotted by natural enemies such as birds and lizards.

Moths' antennae are straight or fernlike. They are used for smelling out nectar, or other moths at night.

The South American ghost moth has the biggest wingspan of any moth. Wingtip to wingtip, it can measure up to 30 cm.

Wings At Rest

One way to tell a moth from a butterfly is to see how the insect folds its wings. Most moths rest with their wings folded over their backs. But butterflies close their wings upright.

Nymphalid butterfly

White ermine moth

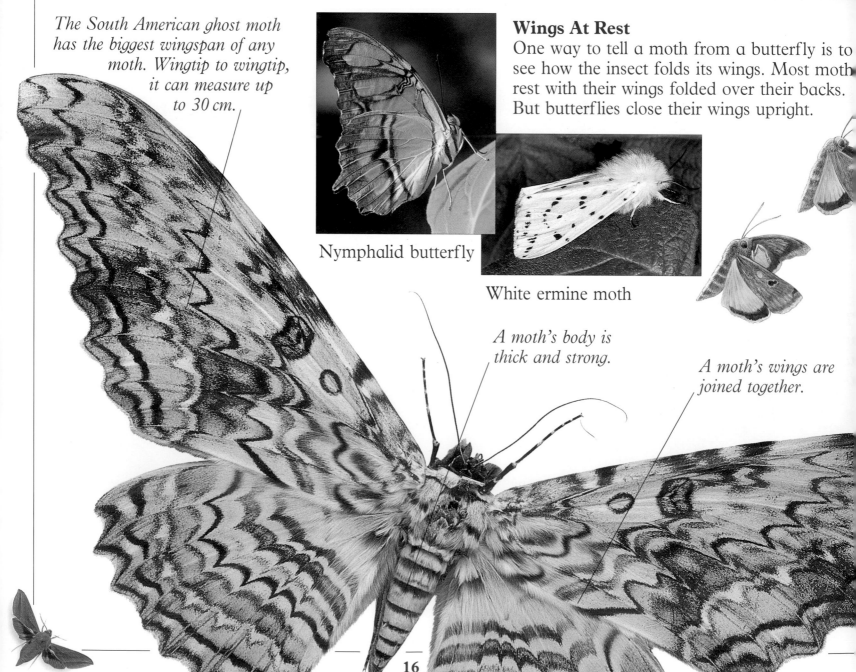

A moth's body is thick and strong.

A moth's wings are joined together.

Whooosss Whooo?

To scare off enemies, like birds, the wing patterns of some moths mimic the appearance of fierce animals. The great peacock moth has big eyespots on its wings which look like an owl's eyes. With these staring back at them, birds think twice before attacking!

Colombian blue wing moth

Madagascan red-tailed moth

A Real Eyeful!

Pyraustine moths have strange feeding habits. With their long proboscises, they drink the tears of animals such as cows and buffaloes. They are so gentle, that the animal's eye does not become irritated.

Verdant hawk-moth

Sloan's uraniid moth

The veins of the moth's wing help to warm or cool the insect.

Spot the Moth!

This geometrid moth from the jungles of Borneo looks like lichen on a tree trunk. The secret of its camouflage is not just colour, but ragged outlines and broken patterns.

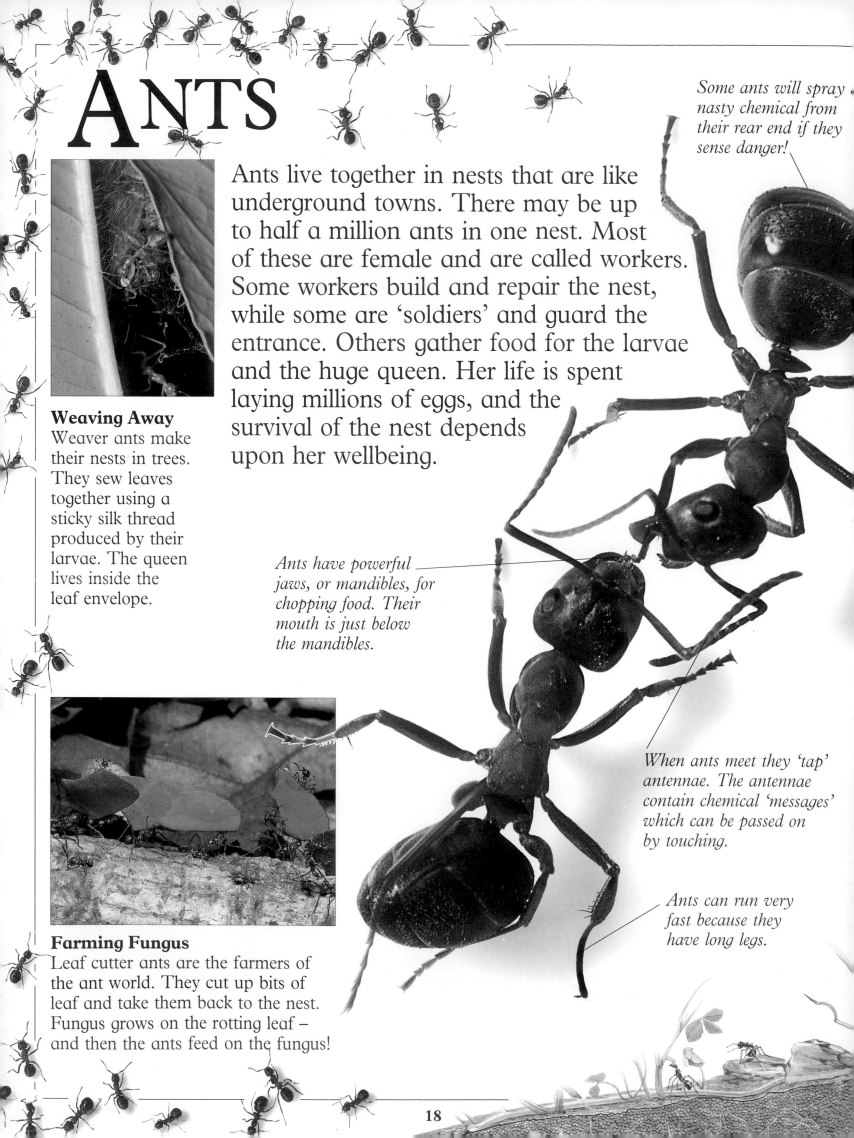

ANTS

Ants live together in nests that are like underground towns. There may be up to half a million ants in one nest. Most of these are female and are called workers. Some workers build and repair the nest, while some are 'soldiers' and guard the entrance. Others gather food for the larvae and the huge queen. Her life is spent laying millions of eggs, and the survival of the nest depends upon her wellbeing.

Some ants will spray nasty chemical from their rear end if they sense danger!

Weaving Away
Weaver ants make their nests in trees. They sew leaves together using a sticky silk thread produced by their larvae. The queen lives inside the leaf envelope.

Ants have powerful jaws, or mandibles, for chopping food. Their mouth is just below the mandibles.

When ants meet they 'tap' antennae. The antennae contain chemical 'messages' which can be passed on by touching.

Ants can run very fast because they have long legs.

Farming Fungus
Leaf cutter ants are the farmers of the ant world. They cut up bits of leaf and take them back to the nest. Fungus grows on the rotting leaf – and then the ants feed on the fungus!

Left, Right!

Driver ants from South America are very fierce insects. They are nomadic, which means they are always on the move. They march in columns through the forest, killing and eating everything in their path. Here they are raiding a wasp's nest.

Living Larders

Some honeypot ant workers spend their whole lives feeding on nectar. Their abdomens swell and when food is hard to find, other workers use them as a food supply.

Bustling Ants

Red ant

Black ant

Harvester Ant

Wood ant

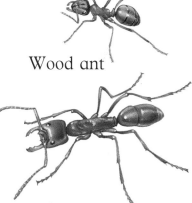

Dinoponera – the largest ant

Inside an Ant's Nest

The success of an ant's nest relies on the hardworking and organized inhabitants.

A network of tunnels joins the chambers in the ant's nest.

Wingless workers take care of the ant larvae.

The queen lays her eggs in the royal chamber.

Seed crusher ant

Soldier ant guarding the entrance

TERMITES

The top of this 'chimney' has a hole in it. This can be made bigger, or smaller, to control the nest temperature.

Within the insect world, termites are the master builders. Their nests are marvels of construction, specially shaped to suit the environment in which they live, whether that is the desert or the rainforest. Up to seven million termites may live together in one nest, which can be a towering mound of mud and soil seven and a half metres high.

Time for Lunch

This anteater has food on its mind. Anteaters don't just eat ants, they eat termites too. They have strong claws which they use to open nests and mounds. Their long snouts make it easy for them to reach the insects inside.

Inside the nest, fungus grows on the termite dung. Termites feed on the fungus. These areas are called fungus gardens.

Food for the inhabitants of the nest is stored in special food galleries.

Deep inside each nest lives a royal couple. Their job is to keep the numbers of the nest as large as possible. The queen lays all the eggs and the king fertilizes them.

Beneath each tower there is a cave that houses dozens of chambers. The cave can be up to 3 metres wide.

Special Jobs

The nests are well organized and each termite has a special job to do. Not all termites look the same – it all depends on what their job is. For example, the workers, who feed and clean the king and queen, are always blind and wingless. The soldiers, who defend them, have strong biting jaws.

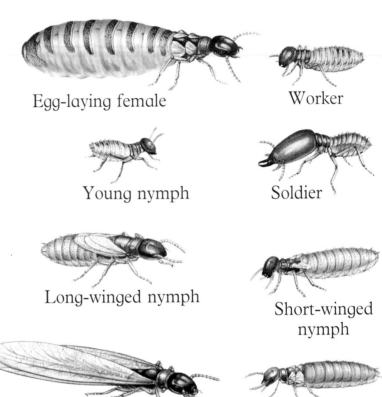

Egg-laying female   Worker

Young nymph   Soldier

Long-winged nymph

Short-winged nymph

Male   Young female

Meet the Queen

This may look like a giant sausage but it is really a queen termite. The queen is the largest termite in the nest. Her body is bloated and full of eggs. She will lay up to 30,000 eggs a day – that's about one egg every three seconds.

The walls of the nest become hard and baked by the Sun.

Workers bring food to the growing larvae.

Home Sweet Home

Termites build their nests to fit in with their surroundings. In Northern Australia, magnetic termites build high, wedge-shaped mounds that run north to south. This means that the scorching midday sun shines on the knife-edged part and the nest does not overheat.

Magnetic nest   Tree nest

Below the main cave are cavities sometimes up to 10 metres deep. The termites' water supply comes from these cavities.

Living in the Jungle

Termites often plaster their nests to trees, high above the ground. In these same jungles, termites build umbrella-shaped nests. The sloping roof protects the nest from heavy rainfall.

Umbrella nest

GRASSHOPPERS

Grasshoppers are known for the 'ticking' sounds they make and for their ability to leap high into the air. There are more than 20,000 different kinds of grasshopper in the world. Grasshoppers are plant-eaters, feeding on leaves and stems. Normally, they prefer to be alone. But under special conditions, they undergo a series of physical changes. They increase in size, become more brightly coloured and gather in their millions to become a swarm of hungry locusts.

The long back legs are good for leaping. A grasshopper can jump over one metre.

Its legs and feet have spikes which it uses to defend itself against enemies.

Grasshoppers have very keen eyesight and hearing.

Grasshoppers' colours help them to blend in with their background.

Name That Tune

Grasshoppers are good fiddle players. They make music the same way a violin produces sound. The grasshopper's leg is its bow and the tough wing vein is the string. Crickets are also known for their musical ability. They use their wings to make sound. One wing has a thick vein with bumps on it. This is called the file. The cricket rubs the file over a rough ridge on the other wing to make cricket music.

Cricket

Grasshopper

Chirping Cousins

Crickets belong to the same insect group as grasshoppers. But crickets have longer antennae and like eating other insects.

Growing Up

Female locusts lay their eggs in the sand. The babies, called nymphs, hatch and dig their way out. When they appear, they are tiny versions of their parents. In order to become fully grown adults, the nymphs moult between three and five times. After each moult the nymphs are bigger than before. When they moult for the final time, they emerge with full-sized wings.

Nymph crawling out of nest

Adult pulling itself free of skin

Adult resting while its wings harden

The Trouble with Locusts

When heavy rains fall in hot, dry regions, lush plant life begins to grow. With lots of food, large numbers of grasshoppers get together to mate. After mating, they eat all the plant life around them and grow much larger. In search of more food they take to the air in huge swarms, devouring fields of valuable crops.

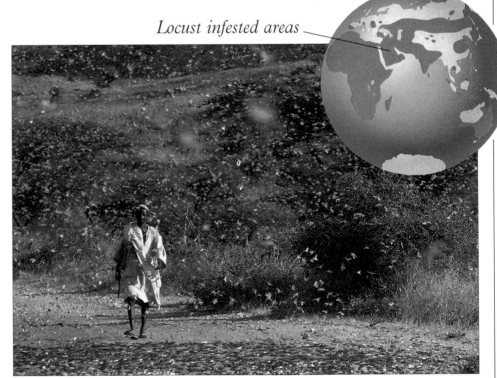

Locust infested areas

Extended Family

All of these insects are related to grasshoppers but they have quite different features – and very clever disguises.

Leaf insect

Stick insect

Praying mantis

BEES

Bumble bee

You have probably heard the buzz of a honeybee as it flies from flower to flower. During the spring and summer months, bees spend their time collecting food. There are thousands of different types of bees and many of them live alone. But social bees, like honeybees, live in large nests or hives. They gather nectar to be stored in the hive and turned into honey.

Nest Making
Some bees make their hives out of chewed leaves, mud and animal hairs.

Working Hives
Man-made hives are specially made to house thousands of bees. Farmers place these hives in their orchards so the bees will pollinate the trees.

As the honeybee moves from flower to flower, a yellow powder on the flower, called pollen, sticks to its body. The bee carries the pollen back to the hive where it is turned into food.

This honeybee is feeding on nectar, a sweet liquid found in flowers. It sucks out the nectar with its long, tube-like mouthparts.

Bees help to pollinate flowers by carrying pollen from flower to flower.

The bee's sting is in its tail.

24

African killer bee

Orchid bee

Parasitic bee

Asian carpenter bee

Honeycomb
Inside the hive, the bees store honey in a comb, which is made up of thousands of little six-sided cells. The bees feed on the honey during the cold winter months.

A large hive can hold up to 50,000 bees.

Worker honeybees look after the young and turn nectar into another sweet liquid we call honey.

Shall we Dance?
Worker bees scout for food. When they find a good supply they do a dance – in a figure of eight pattern – to tell the other bees where the food is. The bees in the hive then know where the food is by the angle of the 'figure of eight' and the position of the sun in the sky.

Queen Bee
Every hive needs a queen. The queen bee mates with the male, called a drone. She then lays all the eggs. New hives are formed in summer when a young queen leads lots of workers out of the old hive to a new one.

Royal Jelly
Royal jelly is actually bees' milk. It is filled with good things like sugar, protein and vitamins. The worker bee larvae do not get to eat the royal food – they are fed on pollen and honey. Only the honeybee larvae that are destined to become queens eat royal jelly. Because it is so rich in vitamins and proteins, people now use it to make face creams, soap and vitamin tablets.

Royal jelly products

WASPS

We know that a bee makes honey, but what does its relative the wasp do? Like bees, wasps help to pollinate plant life. Many wasps spend their lives eating the grubs and caterpillars of insects that are harmful to important food crops. Some wasps like company and live together in nests with thousands of other wasps. But many wasps live alone. They are called solitary wasps.

Home in a Root
Gall wasps lay eggs in oak roots. A swelling, called a gall, grows around the developing larva and provides it with food and protection.

American wasp

Wasps have sense hairs on their heads which give information about their surroundings.

Wasps use their antennae to measure the size and shape of each new cell in the nest as it is built.

This wing is actually made up of two wings joined together by a tiny row of 'hooks'. The hooks allow it to work as one wing.

Wasps have powerful jaws. They use them for digging, cutting and making their nest.

The common wasp is between 15 and 20 millimetres long.

Wasps have a narrow waist which separates their thorax and abdomen.

The Busy Potter
The female potter wasp is really quite artistic. To house and protect her egg, she builds a delicate little pot made of mud. Then she finds food for the egg and places it inside the pot. After laying her egg she seals the nest.

The female puts a caterpillar in the pot.

When the larva hatches, it has a safe home and lots of food.

Paper Homes

The common wasp's nest is made from chewed wood fibres mixed with saliva – which makes a material much like paper. To begin with, the queen works on her own, building several layers around the egg cells in the centre. Then she lays eggs in each cell. When the eggs hatch, the newly born workers help the queen to finish the nest.

The queen wasp is beginning the nest.

The bright yellow and black stripes are a warning to predators to keep away – or else!

A nest of common wasps can be 45 centimetres wide.

A wasp's sting is in its tail.

Parasitic wasp

Giant wood wasp

Paper wasp

Watch Out for that Sting

Only the queen and worker wasps have a sting. They use their sting as a defence against predators and to paralyze prey.

Tarantula for Dinner

The tarantula hawk wasp is the world's largest wasp. The female catches tarantulas and stuns them with her sting. She puts the tarantula in a burrow and lays her eggs on it. When the young hatch, they have a tasty meal.

WATER INSECTS

Walking beside a pond, on a calm summer evening, you might not notice much sign of life. But if you were to look more closely, you would find a world swarming with insects. Many insects live close to watery areas – such as ponds, rivers and lakes – and many more live just on the surface. But there are also thousands of insects that live under the water. In fact, many insects pass from one stage of their development to another, in the water.

Water measurer

The water boatman uses its hind legs like oars.

The water boatman swims along upside down in the water and pops up to the surface to breathe.

Its front legs are strong and made for grasping.

The bug's hairy legs help it to swim.

Whirligig beetles can fly, swim on the surface and dive under water.

This great diving beetle is a fierce hunter of small fish and insects. It can stay in the water a long time by storing air under its wings.

Midge larva

This damselfly nymph is almost ready to leave the water to spend the rest of its life in the air.

The fringes on the beetle's legs help to push it through the water.

Mayfly nymphs eat plants and breathe through feathery gills on their abdomen.

Caddis fly larvae make a protective shell out of silk, twigs and little stones.

Midges are tiny flies.
They fly in large swarms
near watery areas.

Pond-skaters do not just walk on
water, they run and jump too!
Their light weight is supported by
an invisible 'skin' which forms on
the surface of the water.

I'll Eat My House
The brown china mark
moth caterpillar builds a
safe, snug home in a water
plant – then it eats it.
It uses the pieces of water
lily leaves to make a shelter
to live in while its body
changes from a caterpillar to a
moth. As it is changing, its house
provides an excellent food supply!

Saucer bugs can
breathe under water
because they have a
silvery film
of air around
their body.

Before a
water beetle
becomes a beetle, it is
a larva. It breathes by
drawing air into large
breathing tubes
in its tail.

Mosquitoes lay batches
of up to 300 eggs in the
water. Tiny worm-like
larvae hatch out from the
eggs. The larvae move
through the water
by wriggling.

These dragonfly eggs
are surrounded by a
protective, sticky jelly.
Tiny dragonfly
nymphs hatch from
the eggs.

Water
scorpion

Dragonfly
nymphs will stay
under water for two
to three years before
they are developed enough
to begin their brief
adult life.

Water beetle pupa

29

DRAGONFLIES

Many insects are good fliers but dragonflies are truly the champions of flight. Millions of years ago, man-sized dragonflies patrolled the skies. Even today's finger-length dragonflies are quite large compared to other insects. Once dragonflies have emerged from their water-based nymph stage, they take to the air, flying at speeds of up to 56 kilometres per hour.

Wing Power
Dragonflies have stron muscles which control the base of the wings. In flight, the wings loc like a rapidly changing X shape.

Dancing Dragonflies
To attract a mate, swarms of male dragonflies perform dances in the air.

Mating dragonflies

Each pair of clear, veined wings can beat separately. This means that dragonflies can hover.

Dragonflies have excellent eyesight. They have two huge compound eyes. Each eye can have up to 30,000 lenses.

Baby Dragonflies
When the female is ready to lay her eggs, she dips her abdomen into the water. The eggs sink below the surface.

The bristles on the dragonfly's front legs help it to trap prey in the air.

Growing up
Once the fully developed dragonfly nymph has climbed up out of the water, it begins its last and most spectacular change. The nymph's skin cracks open and an adult dragonfly pulls itself free.

Beautiful Friends

The delicately beautiful damselfly and mayfly are related to the powerful dragonfly. They also spend most of their lives under water, as nymphs. When they become adults, they have a short time to live. In that time they must mate and lay eggs so that the next generation can develop.

Mayfly

Damselfly

When dragonflies are at rest, their wings are fully open.

Dragonflies are usually very brightly coloured. Their bodies are long and slender.

Mighty Dragonflies

Flat-bodied 'darter' dragonfly

Emperor dragonfly

Club tail dragonfly

Common darter dragonfly

COCKROACHES

Cockroaches can survive almost anywhere, feeding on almost anything. That is why they are one of the oldest types of winged insect in the world. They have existed on Earth about one hundred times longer than people. They are often called the rats and mice of the insect world because they like our warm, sheltered homes and feed on the rubbish we throw away.

A Crawler with Wings
Did you know that cockroaches can actually fly? Here you can see the cockroach's wing-case.

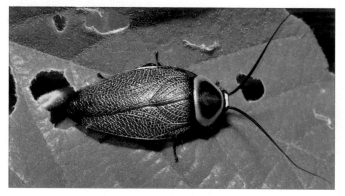

Warning Colours
This South American cockroach is mimicking the colour pattern of a poisonous beetle. Birds will therefore avoid eating it.

Cockroaches are very sensitive to vibrations – they can sense a movement of less than one-millionth of a millimetre.

The female produces a hard egg purse, called an ootheca, to carry her eggs in. Inside the purse are two rows of eggs.

Wing-case

Cockroaches have tail feelers, called cerci, at the end of their abdomen. These are very sensitive to touch.

Their spiny legs are used to fight off predators.

Hidden Away

Most cockroaches never bother us at all. They live in all sorts of environments, such as tropical forests, caves, deserts, and under the ground.

Madagascan hissing cockroach

Rainforest cockroach

Desert cockroach

American cockroach

Oriental cockroach

Greedy Insects

Cockroaches are scavengers. Many of them live on plant life but others are happy to eat the kinds of food we like to eat! Some will even eat man-made things such as paper.

Cockroaches eating cake

Cockroaches eating paper packaging

Their long, thread-like antennae help them to feel their way in the dark.

Safety in Numbers

These cockroach nymphs are sticking together. The larger the group, the more protection there is for the individual nymph. Also, the bright colours on their bodies trick birds and lizards into thinking that they are either poisonous or taste horrible!

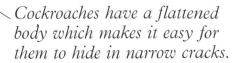

Cockroaches have a flattened body which makes it easy for them to hide in narrow cracks.

WEB SPIDERS

Spiders are different from insects in many ways. Firstly, they have a different name – they are called arachnids. Unlike insects, their head and thorax are fused together. They have four pairs of walking legs and no antennae. All spiders are meat-eaters. Some spiders, like this funnel web spider, make webs to catch their prey.

I'll Eat You Later
If a web spider catches a tasty insect, but is not hungry, it poisons it but does not kill it. Then it wraps it in silk and keeps it for later.

Up, Up and Away
When baby spiders – called spiderlings – want to travel long distances they take to the air. They do not have wings but they are still able to fly. They produce a piece of silk and use it like a balloon.

Spiders do not have bones. Their head and thorax are covered by a hardened shield.

The spiderling suspends itself from a long line.

It makes a loop which is slowly drawn up by the breeze.

When it's ready to take off, it cuts itself free.

Silk is produced through the spinnerets on the end of the spider's abdomen. Spiders use their legs to pull the silk out.

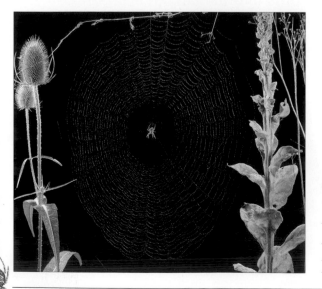

Garden Surprise
Scientists think that insects are attracted to spiders' webs because the webs reflect ultraviolet light. Insects use ultraviolet light to find their way and to find food.

The sac-like abdomen contains the heart, lung, silk glands and the reproductive parts.

Ready to Attack

This Australian funnel web spider is one of the world's deadliest. Here it is poised, ready to attack! When spiders catch their prey, usually insects, they use their 'fangs' to poison and kill them. The funnel web spider, like most spiders, uses its strong digestive juices to dissolve the insect's insides so the spider can suck it dry.

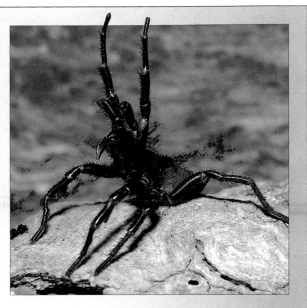

Spiders and Webs

The net-casting spider lives in trees, mostly in jungle areas. To catch prey, it spins a sticky net and throws it over passing insects.

The water spider spins a web in the shape of a bell under the water. It fills the bell with a bubble of air and moves in.

Most web spiders have eight simple eyes, called ocelli. But even so, they cannot see very well.

Making a Web

Making a web takes time and special care. Spiders only spin new webs when the old ones become untidy or damaged.

Spiders have a pair of graspers, called palps, on each side of their mouthparts. They are used to seize prey.

The web of the orb web spider looks like a target. It takes about an hour to spin a complete web.

Spiders have eight legs.

The female purse web spider lives in a silken pouch. When an unsuspecting insect lands on top, the spider bites through the pouch and grabs it.

Even though spiders do not have ears, they can 'listen' to the world around them through their webs. The webs are very sensitive to vibrations in the air.

HUNTING SPIDERS

Not all spiders spin a web and wait for their prey to get caught in it. Many catch their prey without the use of silk. They are called hunting spiders. Some patrol their territory looking for insects to pounce on. Others crouch in burrows and wait for prey to wander past. Unlike web spiders, hunting spiders have strong jumping legs and keen eyesight so that they can easily spot their victims.

This Chilean red-leg spider is one of the largest hunting spiders in the world. It is more than five inches from leg to leg. It hunts at night and eats mice and birds.

A hunting spider has eight simple eyes on the front of its head. It hardly has to move its head to be able to see in all directions.

Hide and Seek

Tree-trunk trapdoor spiders are tricky creatures. After they have made a safe, secure burrow with their powerful jaws, they construct a trapdoor at the entrance. Unseen, they lie in wait behind the trapdoor, ready to leap upon any unsuspecting insects that might crawl by.

The hairs on the spider's body are very sensitive to vibrations made by moving prey.

It has strong legs for digging burrows.

Brazilian wandering spider

Long Jumpers

Hunting spiders need good eyesight because they have to see and chase after their next meal. Many can measure exactly the leap they must make onto their victim, as they run along after it.

Crab spider

Full Speed Ahead

Wolf spiders hunt during the day. This Australian wolf spider lurks at the entrance of its silk-lined tunnel ready to race full speed after prey.

Raft spider

Woodlouse spider

Take Aim, Fire!

Spitting spiders spit when they are hungry. When they spot an insect, they spit streams of sticky gum from each fang. This glues the insect to the ground until the spider can arrive to eat it.

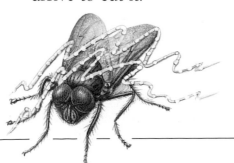

SCORPIONS

Scorpions are known to be deadly. But their reputation is worse than their sting. Like spiders, scorpions are arachnids. They live mostly in hot countries – in deserts or rainforests. They are shy creatures, spending their days in burrows where it is cool. They have even been known to creep into people's shoes to get out of the sun.

I'm Not Afraid of You
Meerkats think scorpions are rather tasty. When they catch a scorpion, they bite off its stinging tail and devour the meaty part of the scorpion's body.

The tail is jointed so that it can bend.

The poison is stored in two glands in the swollen part of the sting.

The sting tip is very sharp for piercing the skin of prey.

Scorpions have four pairs of simple eyes but they rely more on smell than on sight.

This is a South African creeping scorpion. Its colour helps it to blend in with its background.

The front legs of scorpions are armed with pincers. These are used to grab and hold prey.

Stinging Scorpions

Imperial scorpion

Bark scorpion

Slender-tailed scorpion

Whip scorpion

Fat-tailed scorpion

Female scorpions, such as this Costa Rican forest scorpion, watch over their young for the first few days of their lives. When the young hatch from their eggs, the female lets them climb up and ride on its back.

Two to Tango

Before scorpions mate they do a special dance. The male grabs the female by the pincers and they move together backwards and forwards. After mating, the male has to beat a hasty retreat in case it is eaten alive by the female!

Desert Food

Desert scorpions can survive without water for several months, and without food for more than a year. When they do catch prey, they pick it to pieces and suck out all its juices! They eat a wide variety of insects.

Desert cricket

Desert wasp

Desert beetle

Desert scorpion

Desert locusts

CENTIPEDES AND MILLIPEDES

Centipedes and millipedes have an external skeleton like insects, but in other ways are very different. Their body does not divide into a separate head and thorax and they do not have wings. Above all, they are many-legged creatures and can have anything from nine to two hundred pairs of legs. You would think that, with so many legs, they might occasionally trip over. But they have amazing control over every single leg.

Walk this Way
Millipede means 'one thousand feet', but no millipede has more than 400 feet. Millipedes move with a slow, wave-like motion, using up to 22 pairs of legs.

Curled Up
The giant African millipede coils itself up into a tight ball when it feels threatened. By curling up it protects the soft underside of its body.

A millipede's body is divided into segments. Each segment has two pairs of legs.

The hard outer skin is called a cuticle.

Millipedes have a row of stink glands along the sides of their bodies.

Pill millipede

Giant millipede

Forward, March
The name centipede means 'one hundred feet'. Centipedes move along very rapidly with less than half their legs touching the ground at any one time.

Plant-Eaters
Millipedes only eat plants. They burrow through the soil, using their strong jaws to scrape and chew rotting leaves.

Meat-Eaters
Centipedes are fierce hunters. They eat grubs, insects and worms. They have even been known to eat lizards, mice and toads.

Like a millipede, a centipede's body is divided up into segments. But each segment has only a single pair of legs.

When they first hatch, centipedes have fewer legs. As they grow bigger, they develop more legs.

The centipede's narrow body allows it to squeeze through small spaces in the soil.

Antenna

Wire worm

The spiny rear legs are for defence.

Poisonous Claws
Centipedes paralyze prey with poison claws that are under their heads.

Cave centipede

Tiger centipede

41

INSECTS IN THE HOME

Even though you may not see them, there are probably insects in your home. They like the warmth, shelter and food a house can provide. Most are not harmful to us, just annoying. But some are so dirty, they may cause illnesses. Others can eat away at the structure of our homes, weakening roofs, floors and stairs.

Silverfish
Silverfish are often found in kitchens. They are actually quite useful in that they eat up any small bits of food we drop in our homes.

Evil Weevil
The grain weevil is actually a beetle. In many parts of the world it is a serious pest because it eats its way through large amounts of stored grain.

Flour Beetles
These beetles are quite often found in people's kitchens eating their way through bags of flour.

Barklice
Barklice usually live under bark on trees. They live on the small moulds that grow there. But they have been known to eat books too!

Woodworm
Woodworm are not actually worms – they are the larvae of beetles. The beetles lay their eggs mostly on wooden furniture. When the eggs hatch, the larvae burrow into the wood.

Flea Larvae
The tiny white flea larvae live on bits of old food found on rugs and carpets.

Holy Jumper!
Some moths lay their eggs on our clothes and in our rugs and carpets. When the eggs hatch the larvae eat the material. That is why the clothes in our wardrobes sometimes end up with holes in them.

Bedbugs
These bugs do not just live in beds, they also live in cracks in walls and furniture. They creep out in the dead of night to feed on human blood.

Cat Fleas
These fleas make their home in the animal's fur, feeding on its blood. Whenever they get the chance, they will leap onto another cat.

Jumping Fleas
Fleas are wingless. But when a flea jumps it is able to launch itself into space with about 20 times the acceleration of an Apollo moon rocket. At rest, a flea's rear legs are like coiled-up springs. These 'springs' are triggered off by tiny elastic structures positioned above them – and the flea is shot forward.

INSECTS THAT SPREAD DISEASE

Throughout history, diseases spread by insects have caused the deaths of millions of people. Today, in many parts of the world, the bite of an insect is no longer such a serious problem. We now have medicines which can cure many previously incurable illnesses. But there are still some places, such as the tropics, where insects can be a serious threat to people's health. When you go out hiking in wooded areas, it is best to tuck your trousers into your boots and wear long sleeves to avoid being bitten by insects.

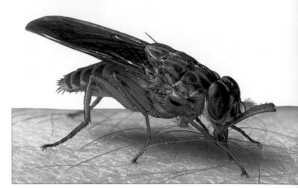

Sleeping Sickness
The African tsetse fly drinks human and animal blood, spreading a disease called sleeping sickness. First this causes extreme tiredness, then it affects the body's nervous system.

Poison Kiss
The South American triatoma bug (sometimes called the kissing bug) causes a skin complaint called Chagas' disease. The infected person develops large, dark patches on his skin.

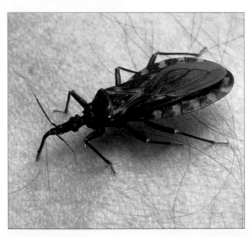

The Body Louse
Lice are bloodsuckers. There are three kinds of lice that live on humans, but the most common is the body louse. It lives on people's clothes and spreads a disease called typhus. Typhus causes severe aches and pains.

Keep Out!
Nets are draped over beds in the tropics so that people can sleep without being bitten by mosquitoes. This simple measure has saved many lives.

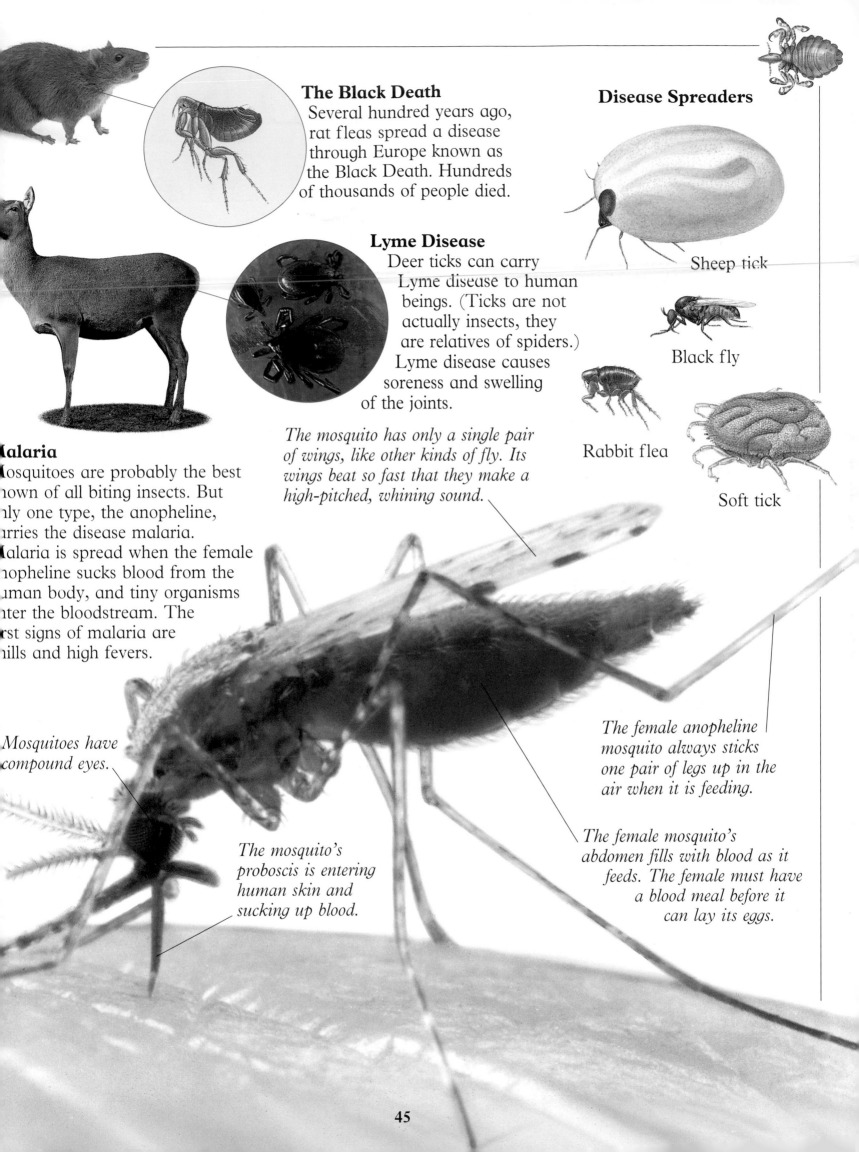

The Black Death

Several hundred years ago, rat fleas spread a disease through Europe known as the Black Death. Hundreds of thousands of people died.

Lyme Disease

Deer ticks can carry Lyme disease to human beings. (Ticks are not actually insects, they are relatives of spiders.) Lyme disease causes soreness and swelling of the joints.

Disease Spreaders

Sheep tick

Black fly

Rabbit flea

Soft tick

Malaria

Mosquitoes are probably the best known of all biting insects. But only one type, the anopheline, carries the disease malaria. Malaria is spread when the female anopheline sucks blood from the human body, and tiny organisms enter the bloodstream. The first signs of malaria are chills and high fevers.

The mosquito has only a single pair of wings, like other kinds of fly. Its wings beat so fast that they make a high-pitched, whining sound.

Mosquitoes have compound eyes.

The female anopheline mosquito always sticks one pair of legs up in the air when it is feeding.

The mosquito's proboscis is entering human skin and sucking up blood.

The female mosquito's abdomen fills with blood as it feeds. The female must have a blood meal before it can lay its eggs.

INSECTS AND MAN

We do not usually think about the number of insects crawling around our world. That is probably just as well, as scientists think that for every person there are about 200 million insects. Insect numbers have been affected by both natural and man-made pest controls. But there is no doubt that they have proved themselves to be formidable survivors.

Moving Overseas
Insects have been accidentally carried all over the world in cargo ships and planes.

Insect Presents
Without these creeping creatures, our planet would be a place without its wonderful variety of fruits and beautiful flowers.

Cactus Killers
Insects are used to control unwanted plants. In Australia, the prickly pear cactus took over vast areas of farmland. So farmers let loose cactus moth caterpillars. They ate the prickly pear, clearing the land.

Insects in the Food Chain
Insects are an important part of the animal food chain.

The beetle…is eaten by a lizard…which is eaten by a bird…which is eaten by a cat.

Pollution Problem

Insects are being found with wings or bodies that are not properly formed. This is because they have had contact with chemicals that have found their way into the rain and into rivers and lakes.

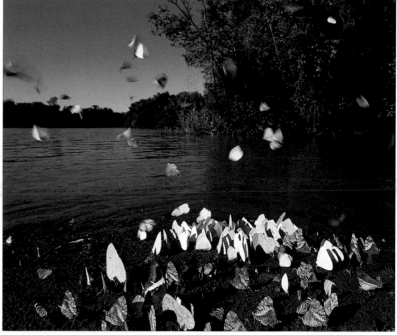

Save our Homes

Like mammals, insects are affected by the destruction of forests and jungles. If their home is threatened, so are they.

Bug Busters

Insects feed on other insects, naturally controlling the numbers. Because many chemical pesticides harm the environment, insects are sometimes used to control other insects. This is called biological control.

Bee Cure

Some insects can provide cures for certain illnesses. Bees' venom is used to treat illnesses which affect the joints and blood circulation, such as rheumatism and arthritis.

GLOSSARY

Abdomen The last of the three sections that make up an insect's body.

Antennae The feelers on an insect's head.

Arachnids Spiders, scorpions and ticks.

Arthropods A group of animals, including insects, with external skeletons.

Biological control A way of keeping down pests by letting other animals loose to feed on them.

Bugs Insects which have beak-like, piercing mouthparts, and wings which are thick at the base and thin at the tip.

Cerci Feelers on an insect's abdomen.

Chrysalis The case inside which a caterpillar turns into a butterfly.

Compound eye An insect eye made up of thousands of tiny lenses.

Cuticle The hard outer skin of an insect.

Environment The surroundings in which an animal lives.

Exoskeleton The skeleton or shell on the outside of an insect's body.

Fertilization The union of male and female cells in order to produce young.

Generation Animals that are born at the same time.

Gland An organ that produces chemicals.

Head The first section of an insect's body.

Halteres The parts of a fly that help it balance in flight.

Hive A house or box for bees to live in.

Larvae The young of insects.

Mandibles Insect jaws.

Mimic To copy the look or behaviour of another animal.

Moult The process of shedding old skin.

Nectar Sugary fluid produced by flowers to attract insects.

Nutrient Any substance needed for growth and health.

Nymph Stage of growth in some insects that comes before adulthood.

Ootheca The egg case of cockroaches and some other insects.

Palps A pair of mouthparts which are used for holding on to food.

Pesticide Chemicals that are used by humans to kill insects.

Pollinate To carry pollen from one flower to another and so fertilize it.

Predator An animal that kills and eats other animals.

Proboscis A tube-shaped mouthpart used for sucking.

Pupa The growth stage that many insect young must go through in order to become adults.

Reproduction The process by which living things produce offspring.

Scavenger An animal that feeds on rotting matter.

Segments The separate sections of an insect's body.

Simple eye An insect eye which has a single, light-sensitive lens.

Spinneret Silk-producing organ in spiders and caterpillars.

Swarm A huge gathering of insects such as bees or locusts.

Thorax The middle section of an insect's body.

Ultraviolet light Light which cannot be detected by the human eye.

Venom Poison that insects and spiders inject into enemies or prey, by biting or stinging.

Vitamins Substances in food that help living things to grow and stay healthy.

Acknowledgments

Photography: Andy Crawford and Dave Rudkin.

Additional photography: Tim Ridley, Jerry Young, Dave King, Frank Greenaway, Kim Taylor, Colin Keates, Jane Burton and Neil Fletcher.

Illustrations: Sandra Doyle, Roy Flooks, Mick Gillah, Norman Lacey, Michael Woods, Richard Manning, Maurice Pledger and Sean Milne.

Models: Donks Models.

Thanks to: John Lane, London School of Hygiene and Tropical Medicine, Scallywags and Norrie Car Child Model Agencies, Caroline Brooke.

b – **bottom**	tc – **top centre**	cra – **centre right above**	clb – **centre left below**
c – **centre**	cb – **centre below**	cla – **centre left above**	crb – **centre right below**
tl – **top left**	bc – **bottom centre**	cr – **centre right**	bl – **bottom left**
tr - **top right**	ca – **centre above.**	cl – **centre left**	br – **bottom right**

INDEX